This Walker book belongs to:

_____

_____

_____

1 •

2 ••

3 •••

4 ••••

5 •••••

6 ••••••

7 •••••••

8

9

10

For Jane W,
with gratitude

First published 2009 as *Olly and Me 123* by Walker Books Ltd
87 Vauxhall Walk, London SE11 5HJ

This edition published 2016

2 4 6 8 10 9 7 5 3 1

© 2009 Shirley Hughes

The right of Shirley Hughes to be identified as author/illustrator of this work
has been asserted by her in accordance with the Copyright, Designs and Patents Act 1988

This book has been typeset in Plantin Light Educational

Printed in China

British Library Cataloguing in Publication Data:
a catalogue record for this book is available from the British Library

ISBN 978-1-4063-7276-2

www.walker.co.uk

THE NURSERY COLLECTION

123

Shirley Hughes

WALKER BOOKS

AND SUBSIDIARIES

LONDON · BOSTON · SYDNEY · AUCKLAND

One is me, Katie.

Here I am, all by myself.

But I'm not by myself for long.
Here comes Olly, my baby brother,
and that makes **two** of us.

2

You need **two** to play a game of hide and seek ...

or a bouncing
game like the
one I play
with Grandpa.

Two things often go together in pairs,
like shoes and socks …

or clashing
saucepan lids …

or these twin babies
who were born on
the very same day.

3 ● ● ●

Three is company
when my friend Norah
comes to play ...

or when our cat Ginger
is in a good mood
and lets us stroke her.

4 ● ● ● ●

My friend Norah's cat has
four dear little kittens.
Each of them has
four neat white paws.

There are **four** people in our family. When we go out we usually take our dog Buster too and that makes **five**. Buster likes to chase birds, but he never catches any.

5 • • • • •

Five fingers on each hand
are very useful for counting.

And here are
five falling leaves …

and **five** friends
meeting in the park.

5 ●●●●

Five of us do ballet together:
Amanda and James and Kim and
Norah and me.

But when Olly
tries to join in,
there are **six**.

6 ●●●●●●

There are **six** of us when Grandma and Grandpa come to visit.

And when I give my own special tea party
in the garden there are **six** of us too.

Buster is allowed to come as long as
he doesn't try to lick the plates.

7

Here are:

seven
slithering
sliders …

seven swift runners …

and **seven**
stylish
hats.

And here are **eight** busy bouncers.

9

Eight children and one big brown dog make **nine**.

Is the **ninth** brick going to
make my tower fall down?

Yes! But never mind!

10 ●●●●●●●●●●●

Ten people
on a
crowded bus.
But hooray!
Here's one
kind gentleman
giving us
his seat.

Some things are too many to count –
like blossoms falling from a tree
or raindrops into a puddle …

or flowers
in the
springtime
or clouds
in the sky
going up
and up…

Numbers
go on
forever.

1 •

2 ••

3 •••

4 ••••

5 •••••

6 ••••••

7 •••••••

8 ●●●●●●●●

9 ●●●●●●●●●

10 ●●●●●●●●●●